INITIAL
VOCALS

Published by
Trinity College London Press Ltd
trinitycollege.com

Registered in England
Company no. 09726123

Photography by Zute Lightfoot, lightfootphoto.com

Printed in England by Halstan & Co Ltd, Amersham, Bucks

Parental and Teacher Guidance:

The songs in Trinity's Rock & Pop syllabus have been arranged
to represent the artists' original recordings as closely and
authentically as possible. Popular music frequently deals with
subject matter that some may find offensive or challenging.
It is possible that the songs may include material that some
might find unsuitable for use with younger learners.

We recommend that parents and teachers exercise their own
judgement to satisfy themselves that the lyrics of selected
songs are appropriate for the students concerned. As you
will be aware, there is no requirement that all songs in this
syllabus must be learned. Trinity does not associate itself with,
adopt or endorse any of the opinions or views expressed in
the selected songs.

THE EXAM AT A GLANCE

In your exam you will perform a set of three songs and one of the session skills assessments. You can choose the order of your set list.

SONG 1

Choose a song from this book.

SONG 2

Choose *either* a different song from this book
or a song from the list of additional Trinity Rock & Pop arrangements, available at trinityrock.com
or a song you have chosen yourself: this could be your own cover version or a song that you have written. It should be at the same level as the songs in this book and match the parameters at trinityrock.com

SONG 3: TECHNICAL FOCUS

Song 3 is designed to help you develop specific and relevant techniques in performance. Choose one of the technical focus songs from this book, which cover two specific technical elements.

SESSION SKILLS

Choose *either* **playback** *or* **improvising**.

Session skills are an essential part of every Rock & Pop exam. They are designed to help you develop the techniques music industry performers need.

Sample tests are available in our *Session Skills* books and free examples can be downloaded from trinityrock.com

ACCESS ALL AREAS

GET THE FULL ROCK & POP EXPERIENCE ONLINE AT TRINITYROCK.COM

We have created a range of digital resources to support your learning and give you insider information from the music industry, available online. You will find support, advice and digital content on:

- Songs, performance and technique
- Session skills
- The music industry

You can access tips and tricks from industry professionals featuring:

- Bite-sized videos that include tips from professional musicians on techniques used in the songs
- 'Producer's notes' on the tracks, to increase your knowledge of rock and pop
- Blog posts on performance tips, musical styles, developing technique and advice from the music industry

JOIN US ONLINE AT:

 /TRINITYROCKANDPOP    @TRINITY_ROCK    /TRINITYROCKANDPOP   and at TRINITYROCK.COM

CONTENTS

THE AUDIO

Professional demo & backing tracks can be downloaded free, see inside cover for details.

Music preparation and book layout by Andrew Skirrow for Camden Music Services
Music consultants: Nick Crispin, Chris Walters, Christopher Hussey, Donna Rudd
Audio arranged, recorded & produced by Tom Fleming
Vocal arrangements by Jane Watkins & Christopher Hussey

Musicians
Bass: Tom Fleming
Double Bass: Sam Burgess
Drums: George Double
Guitar: Tom Fleming
Vocals: Bo Walton, Brendan Reilly, Emily Barden

TECHNICAL FOCUS

FADE INTO YOU

MAZZY STAR

WORDS AND MUSIC: HOPE SANDOVAL, DAVID ROBACK

INITIAL
VOCALS

SINGLE BY
Mazzy Star

ALBUM
So Tonight That I Might See

B-SIDE
Blue Flower
I'm Gonna Bake My Biscuit

RELEASED
5 October 1993

**12 April 1994
(single)**

LABEL
Capitol

WRITERS
**Hope Sandoval
David Roback**

PRODUCER
David Roback

Californian folk-pop duo Mazzy Star are singer, songwriter and guitarist Hope Sandoval and guitarist, keyboard player, songwriter, producer and former leader of The Rain Parade, David Roback. They have released four highly regarded albums since 1990.

Although never a big hit, the pretty, plaintive 'Fade into You' has become an enduring classic and a favourite for soundtracking emotional scenes in numerous films and TV shows. It is the opening song on the band's second album, *So Tonight that I Might See*, released in 1993. As well as Mazzy Star, Sandoval has provided guest vocals for songs by The Jesus and Mary Chain, The Chemical Brothers, Death in Vegas, Bert Jansch, Air and Massive Attack. She is also half of another duo: Hope Sandoval & the Warm Inventions, formed with My Bloody Valentine drummer and founding member Colm Ó Ciosóig.

TECHNICAL FOCUS

Two technical focus elements are featured in this song:

- Breath control
- Counting

Breath control is important in this song to enable you to sustain each phrase, especially from bar 38 onwards. **Counting** is important too because many notes are placed on the weaker second and third beats of the bar. Count carefully to observe these rhythms.

FADE INTO YOU

WORDS AND MUSIC:
HOPE SANDOVAL, DAVID ROBACK

ANGELS
THE XX

WORDS AND MUSIC: ROMY MADLEY CROFT, OLIVER SIM JAMIE SMITH

SINGLE BY
The xx

ALBUM
Coexist

RELEASED
17 July 2012

RECORDED
**November 2011-May 2012
The xx's studio
London, England (album)**

LABEL
Young Turks

WRITERS
**Romy Madley Croft
Oliver Sim
Jamie Smith**

PRODUCER
Jamie xx

The xx is an English band who released their debut album in 2009, earning them the prestigious Mercury Music Prize the following year. The band's second album *Coexist* debuted at No. 1 in the UK, Belgium, Portugal and Switzerland and No. 5 in the US in 2012.

'Angels' is the opening song and lead single from Coexist, released two months ahead of the album in July 2012. Their most sparse, restrained and intimate number yet, the song was written by the band's Romy Madley Croft (who sings the hushed vocal to her guitar accompaniment), Oliver Sim (who plays bass on the track) and Jamie Smith (who provided the subtle beats and also produced it). Although the song comes first on the album, the band chose it to finish the live sets of their 2013 world tour which included performances at Coachella, Bonnaroo, Glastonbury and Fuji Rock festivals. As well as reaching No. 1, *Coexist* was also the best-selling vinyl album of 2012 in the UK.

⚡ PERFORMANCE TIPS

Most of the phrases in this subtle song do not start on beat 1, so take care to place the first note of each phrase on the correct beat. The melody requires a light breathy delivery with gentle dynamics throughout, and you should aim to capture the tender emotional mood in your performance.

ANGELS

WORDS AND MUSIC:
ROMY MADLEY CROFT,
OLIVER SIM, JAMIE SMITH

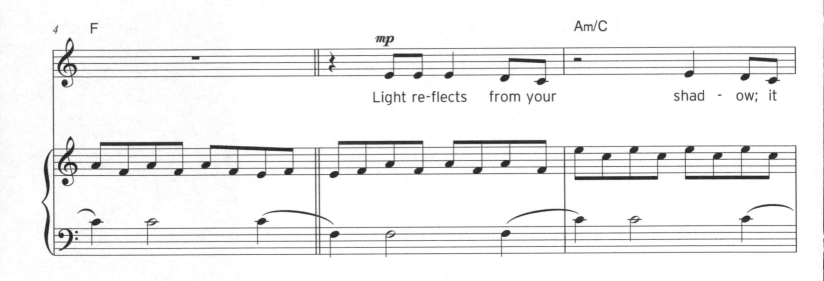

Light re-flects   from your   shad - ow; it

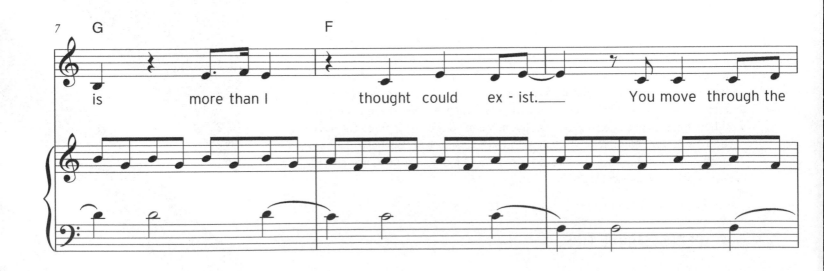

is   more than I   thought could   ex - ist.____   You move through the

TECHNICAL FOCUS

HERE COMES THE SUN

THE BEATLES

WORDS AND MUSIC: GEORGE HARRISON

SINGLE BY
The Beatles

ALBUM
Abbey Road

RELEASED
26 September 1969

RECORDED
7 July–19 August 1969

LABEL
Apple

WRITER
George Harrison

PRODUCER
George Martin

The Beatles – John Lennon, Paul McCartney, George Harrison and Ringo Starr – released their first album, *Please Please Me*, in 1963. Over the course of the next seven years and 12 albums they would change the face of popular music and become the world's best-selling band in the process.

'Here Comes the Sun' is one of two timeless songs Harrison contributed to The Beatles' classic 1969 album *Abbey Road*, the other being 'Something'. This was the last album recorded by The Beatles before their split in 1970 marked Harrison's recognition as a songwriter to rival Lennon and McCartney, something that would be asserted further on his solo album that year, *All Things Must Pass*. Harrison wrote 'Here Comes the Sun' in the garden of his friend Eric Clapton's Surrey country house on one of Clapton's acoustic guitars. Clapton said:

> It was one of those beautiful spring mornings. I think it was April, we were just walking around the garden with our guitars. He was just a magical guy. We sat down at the bottom of the garden, looking out, and the sun was shining. He began to sing the opening lines and I just watched this thing come to life.

TECHNICAL FOCUS

Two technical focus elements are featured in this song:

- Counting
- Syncopation

This well-loved song poses some rhythmic challenges. **Counting** is important – every phrase begins on the second beat, and you will need to place this precisely each time. Within the phrases there is plenty of **syncopation** which is an important aspect of the melody. Aim to replicate the notated rhythms closely while also aiming for a relaxed feel.

TECHNICAL FOCUS

HERE COMES THE SUN

WORDS AND MUSIC: GEORGE HARRISON

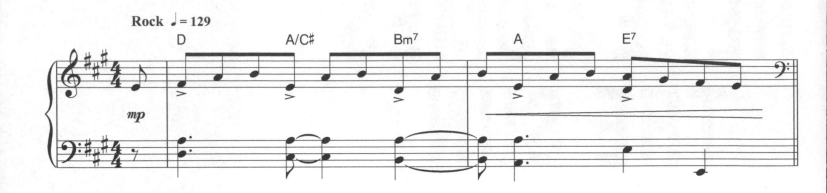

14

KNOCKIN' ON HEAVEN'S DOOR
BOB DYLAN

WORDS AND MUSIC: BOB DYLAN

SINGLE BY
Bob Dylan

ALBUM
Pat Garrett & Billy The Kid

B-SIDE
Turkey Chase

RELEASED
13 July 1973

RECORDED
January-February 1973 (album)

LABEL
Columbia

WRITER
Bob Dylan

PRODUCER
Gordon Carroll

Born in Duluth, Minnesota in 1941, Bob Dylan is often regarded as the most important and influential singer-songwriter in popular music. With a career spanning more than 50 years and a vast catalogue of classic songs, he has been a key influence on artists including The Beatles, Jimi Hendrix, David Bowie and Bruce Springsteen. In 2016 he was awarded the Nobel Prize for Literature.

The timeless 'Knockin' on Heaven's Door' was written by Dylan for director Sam Peckinpah's 1973 film *Pat Garrett and Billy the Kid*, in which Dylan made his big screen acting debut as the character Alias. The song reached No. 14 in the UK and No. 12 in the US, and has become one of Dylan's most covered songs. Eric Clapton took it to the UK top 40 with his reggae-inspired version in 1975, while Guns N' Roses reached No. 2 in the UK with their version in 1992. More recently, Gabrielle's song 'Rise', based on 'Knockin' on Heaven's Door' and featuring extensive sample of the track, topped the UK chart in 2009.

⚡ PERFORMANCE TIPS

There are lots of semiquavers in the melody in this song - take care to sing these with rhythmic precision while maintaining a feel that is not overly rigid. Where phrases begin on the second beat, be sure to count the rest on beat 1. Try to slide the notes together where slurs are written (for example in bar 5) to help create an authentic vocal sound.

KNOCKIN' ON HEAVEN'S DOOR

WORDS AND MUSIC: BOB DYLAN

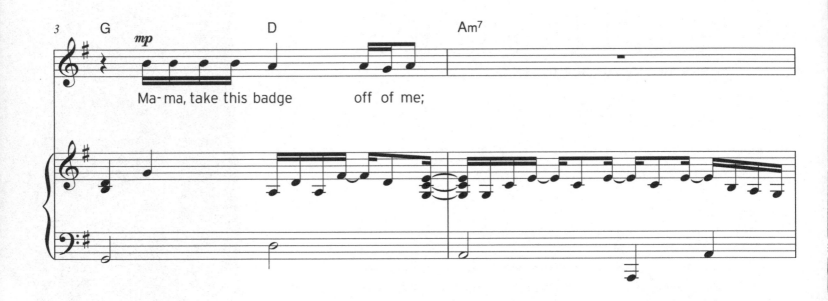

Ma-ma, take this badge off of me;

I can't use it an-y-more.

It's get-tin' dark, too dark__ to see;__

I feel I'm knock-in' on heav-en's door.__

Knock, knock, knock-in' on heav en's door.__

Knock, knock, knock-in' on heav-en's door.

Knock, knock, knock-in' on heav-en's door.

Knock, knock, knock-in' on heav-en's door.

TECHNICAL FOCUS

HOLD ON, WE'RE GOING HOME DRAKE

WORDS AND MUSIC: AUBREY GRAHAM, NOAH SHEBIB
MAJID AL MASKATI, JORDAN ULLMAN

SINGLE BY
Drake

ALBUM
Nothing Was The Same

RELEASED
7 August 2013

RECORDED
**2012-2013
(album)**

LABEL
**OVO Sound
Aspire
Young Money
Cash Money
Republic**

WRITERS
**Aubrey Graham
Noah Shebib
Majid Al Maskati
Jordan Ullman**

PRODUCERS
**Nineteen85
Majid Jordan
Noah "40" Shebib**

Born Aubrey Graham but better known by his middle and stage name Drake, Toronto-born singer, rapper, writer and producer is one of the most successful solo acts of the last decade. All four of his studio albums plus two mixtapes have topped the album charts, both in the US and his native Canada.

The Michael Jackson-influenced 'Hold on, We're Going Home' followed the mainstream success of Drake's 2012 Rihanna-featuring hit 'Take Care'. It became his first top five appearance in both the UK and US charts the following year. Taken from his third album *Nothing Was the Same*, the American online music magazine *Pitchfork* named it No. 1 in their Top 100 Tracks Of 2013 review. Covered many times since, five widely diverse artists have performed the song for BBC Radio 1's popular Live Lounge sessions alone: indie rock band Arctic Monkeys, pop girl group The Saturdays, acoustic singer-songwriter Nick Mulvey, grime artist Stormzy and LA dance pop band Foster the People.

TECHNICAL FOCUS

Two technical focus elements are featured in this song:

- Diction
- Rhythm

The melody of this R&B song is intricate and detailed, requiring close attention to **diction** and **rhythm**. Clear diction will help you make sure that all the words are clearly audible, which you should aim to maintain as the dynamic level increases. To help keep the groove strong, aim for rhythmic accuracy throughout, especially where rhythms are syncopated.

TECHNICAL FOCUS

HOLD ON, WE'RE GOING HOME

WORDS AND MUSIC:
AUBREY GRAHAM, NOAH SHEBIB
MAJID AL MASKATI, JORDAN ULLMAN

hot love _ and e - mo - tion   end - less - ly. _ 'Cause you're a   good girl _ and you know it.

You   act so dif - f'rent a - round me. _   'Cause you're a

good girl _ and you know it.   I   know ex - act - ly who _ you could be.

Just hold on we're go-ing home.

Just hold on we're

go-ing home.

It's hard to do__these things a-lone.__

Just hold on we're go-ing home, ha__ ha ha.

SONGBIRD

OASIS

WORDS AND MUSIC: LIAM GALLAGHER

INITIAL
VOCALS

SINGLE BY
Oasis

ALBUM
Heathen Chemistry

B-SIDE
**(You've Got) The Heart Of
A Star**

Columbia (live)

RELEASED
**1 July 2002 (album)
3 February 2003 (single)**

RECORDED
October 2001-March 2002

**Wheeler End
Buckinghamshire, England**

**Olympic Studios
London, England**

LABEL
Big Brother

WRITER
Liam Gallagher

PRODUCERS
Oasis

From the release of their 1994 debut album *Definitely Maybe*, the UK music scene was dominated by Oasis for the remainder of the decade. Led by Mancunian brothers Noel and Liam Gallagher, the band led the charge of the mid-90s Britpop phenomenon with eight No. 1 albums to their name.

The short and sweet 'Songbird' was the first Oasis song not written by Noel Gallagher to be released as a single, coming from the pen of younger brother and band frontman Liam Gallagher. Liam's only prior songwriting credit had been 'Little James' on the 2000 Oasis album *Standing on the Shoulder of Giants*, while its 2002 follow-up *Heathen Chemistry* (their fifth UK No. 1 album) would feature three by the younger Gallagher, including 'Songbird'. The song reached No. 3 on the UK singles chart in February 2003 and was the band's 15th top-five hit. Clocking in at just over two minutes, it is the shortest of all Oasis singles and also the shortest song to ever appear on the long-running *Now That's What I Call Music!* hit compilation series (appearing on the 54th edition).

⚡ PERFORMANCE TIPS

The melody of this song has several phrases that end with a slur over several notes, for example in bars 42-43. Sliding these notes into each other will help you capture the style of the original. There are also a few melodic jumps, for example the interval of a fourth between bars 6 and 7, which will need to be delivered precisely.

SONGBIRD

WORDS AND MUSIC: LIAM GALLAGHER

dream these kind of things,___ e-spec-ial-ly when she came and spread her wings. Whis-pered in my

ear the things I'd like, then she flew a - way in - to the night._____ Gon-na write a

song so she can see; give her all the love she gives to me. Talk of bet-ter

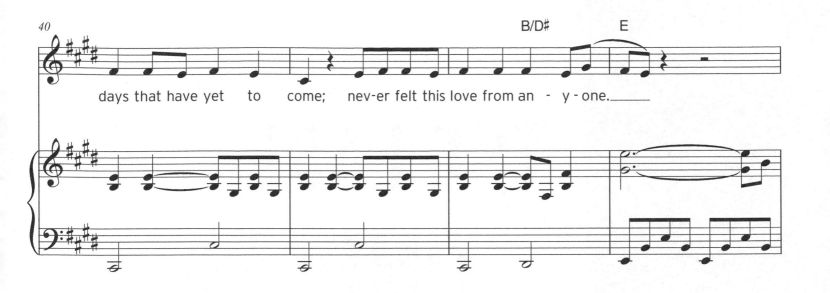

days that have yet to come; nev-er felt this love from an - y - one.___

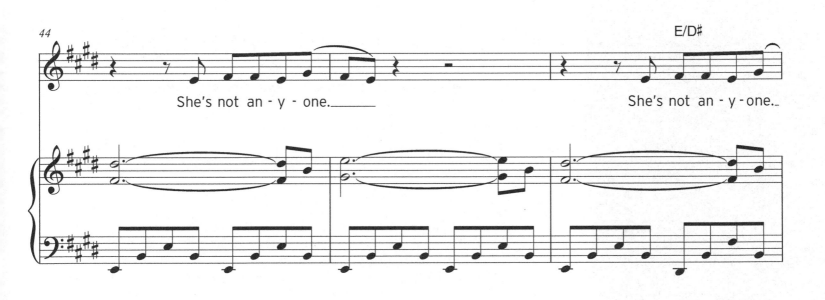

She's not an - y - one.___

She's not an - y - one._

She's not an-y-one.___

INITIAL
VOCALS

SINGLE BY
The Rolling Stones

B-SIDE
Play With Fire

RELEASED
26 February 1965

RECORDED
11-12 January 1965
RCA Studios, Hollywood
Los Angeles, California
USA

LABEL
Decca

WRITERS
Mick Jagger
Keith Richards

PRODUCER
Andrew Loog Oldham

THE LAST TIME THE ROLLING STONES

WORDS AND MUSIC: MICK JAGGER, KEITH RICHARDS

The Rolling Stones is one of the most successful and enduring groups in the history of rock. They formed in London, England in 1962 when childhood friends and future writing partners Mick Jagger (vocals) and Keith Richards (guitar) hooked up with multi-instrumentalist Brian Jones before adding Bill Wyman (bass) and Charlie Watts (drums).

Released in 1965, 'The Last Time' was the first song written by Mick Jagger and Keith Richards to be released as a single and their third UK No. 1 hit (following the covers 'It's All Over Now' and 'Little Red Rooster'). The song had been inspired by a 1950s recording by The Staple Singers of a traditional gospel song called 'This May Be the Last Time'. In the band's 2003 book *According to the Rolling Stones*, Richards said of the song:

> 'The Last Time' was kind of a bridge into thinking about writing for the Stones. It gave us a level of confidence, a pathway of how to do it. And once we had done that we were in the game.

They went on to score five further self-penned No. 1s that decade.

⚡ PERFORMANCE TIPS

The melody of this classic rock song should be performed with a slight swing – perhaps better described as a swagger. The chorus requires a degree of breath control, so be sure to breathe on the rests between the phrases (especially the crotchet rest in bars 24 and 53) to give you enough breath for the long final phrase of the chorus.

THE LAST TIME

WORDS AND MUSIC:
MICK JAGGER, KEITH RICHARDS

'60s Pop, slightly swung ♩ = 82

Well, I told you once__ and I told you twice.__

But you nev - er lis - ten to my ad - vice__

You don't try ve - ry hard___ to please me.

With what you know, it should be ea - sy.

Well, this could be the last time,___

this could be the last time.__ May - be the last time,

I don't know.____ Oh,

no. Oh, no. Well, I'm

Well, this could be the last time,— this could be the last time.— May - be the last time, I don't know.— Oh, no. Oh, no. Oh, no.

INITIAL
VOCALS

SINGLE BY
Bob Marley & The Wailers

ALBUM
Exodus

B-SIDE
Every Need Got An Ego To Feed

RELEASED
3 June 1977 (album)
12 September 1980 (single)

RECORDED
1976, Harry J. Studio
Kingston, Jamaica

January-April 1977 Island
Studios, London England
(album)

LABEL
Tuff Gong
Island Records

WRITER
Bob Marley

PRODUCERS
Bob Marley & The Wailers

THREE LITTLE BIRDS
BOB MARLEY & THE WAILERS

WORDS AND MUSIC: BOB MARLEY

Bob Marley was a Jamaican singer-songwriter and reggae artist who started out as a member of The Wailers with Bunny Wailer and Peter Tosh. The latter two left in 1974, and Marley continued with longstanding rhythm section Aston Barrett (bass) and Carlton Barrett (drums) to become the most successful reggae act of all time.

The penultimate song on Bob Marley and the Wailers' ninth album, 1977's *Exodus*, 'Three Little Birds' wasn't actually released as a single until 1980. Three further albums had been released in the interim: 1978's *Kaya*, 1979's *Survival* and 1980's *Uprising*. It was the fourth of five top-30 hit singles from *Exodus*, following on from 'Waiting in Vain', 'Jamming' and the title track, reaching No. 17 in the UK. It was his last hit while still alive (Marley died in 1981 at the age of 36). One of the song's inspirations came from Marley's backing singers – the I Threes, comprising his wife Rita Marley, Marcia Griffiths and Judy Mowatt, whom he referred to as 'my three little birds'. Three years after his death, the song featured on Marley's greatest hits collection *Legend*, his first No. 1 album in the UK and a multi-million seller that remains the world's best-ever selling reggae album.

 PERFORMANCE TIPS

This upbeat song features some detailed rhythms, including semiquavers and some syncopation. Take care to observe these while also aiming for a relaxed feel. To capture the reggae style, try singing with a slight staccato feel, which will also help emphasise the words.

THREE LITTLE BIRDS

WORDS AND MUSIC: BOB MARLEY

CHOOSING SONGS FOR YOUR EXAM

SONG 1

Choose a song from this book.

SONG 2

Choose a song which is:

Either a different song from this book

or from the list of additional Trinity Rock & Pop arrangements, available at trinityrock.com

or from a printed or online source

or your own arrangement

or a song that you have written yourself

You can perform Song 2 unaccompanied or with a backing track (minus the voice). If you like, you can create a backing track yourself (or with friends), include a live self-played accompaniment on any instrument, or be accompanied live by another musician.

The level of difficulty and length of the song should be similar to the songs in this book and match the parameters available at trinityrock.com

When choosing a song, think about:

- Does it work for my voice?

- Are there any technical elements that are too difficult for me? (If so, perhaps save it for when you do the next grade)

- Do I enjoy singing it?

- Does it work with my other songs to create a good set list?

SONG 3: TECHNICAL FOCUS

Song 3 is designed to help you develop specific and relevant techniques in performance. Choose one of the technical focus songs from this book, which cover two specific technical elements.

SHEET MUSIC

If your choice for Song 2 is not from this book, you must provide the examiner with a photocopy. The title, writers of the song and your name should be on the sheet music. You must also bring an original copy of the book, or a download version with proof of purchase, for each song that you perform in the exam.

Your music can be:

- A lead sheet with lyrics, chords and melody line

- A chord chart with lyrics

- A full score using conventional staff notation

SINGING WITH BACKING TRACKS

All your backing tracks can be downloaded from soundwise.co.uk

- The backing tracks begin with a click track, which sets the tempo and helps you start accurately

- Be careful to balance the volume of the backing track against your voice

- Listen carefully to the backing track to ensure that you are singing in time

If you are creating your own backing track, here are some further tips:

- Make sure that the sound quality is of a good standard

- Think carefully about the instruments/sounds you are using on the backing track

- Avoid copying what you are singing in the exam on the backing track – it should support, not duplicate

- Do you need to include a click track at the beginning?

COPYRIGHT IN A SONG

If you are a singer, instrumentalist or songwriter it is important to know about copyright. When someone writes a song they automatically own the copyright (sometimes called 'the rights'). Copyright begins once a piece of music has been documented or recorded (eg by video, CD or score notation) and protects the interests of the creators. This means that others cannot copy it, sell it, make it available online or record it without the owner's permission or the appropriate licence.

COVER VERSIONS

- When an artist creates a new version of a song it is called a 'cover version'

- The majority of songwriters subscribe to licensing agencies, also known as 'collecting societies'. When a songwriter is a member of such an agency, the performing rights to their material are transferred to the agency (this includes cover versions of their songs)

- The agency works on the writer's behalf by issuing licences to performance venues, who report what songs have been played, which in turn means that the songwriter will receive a payment for any songs used

- You can create a cover version of a song and use it in an exam without needing a licence

There are different rules for broadcasting (eg TV, radio, internet), selling or copying (pressing CDs, DVDs etc), and for printed material, and the appropriate licences should be sought out.

YOUR
PAGE
NOTES

YOUR
PAGE
NOTES